Awakening Afterlife

Lessons from Near-Death Experiences

By: Martin Rincon

Preface: In the Footsteps of Inspiration 10
Introduction: 13
    What is a near-death experience (NDE)? 13
    How common are NDEs? 14
    What are the different types of NDEs? 14
    What are the most common elements of NDEs? 15
    Why are NDEs important? 15
Chapter 2: The Science of NDEs 17
    What does brain science tell us about NDEs? 17
    Can NDEs be explained by hallucinations or other medical conditions? 18
    What are the implications of NDEs for our understanding of consciousness and death? 20
Chapter 3: The Stories of NDEs 22
    First-hand accounts of NDEs from people from all walks of life 22
    The impact of NDEs on people's lives 23
    The lessons that people have learned from their NDEs 24
Chapter 4: The Truth About NDEs 26
    What can we learn from NDEs about the afterlife? 26
    Do NDEs provide evidence for a soul or consciousness beyond the body? 27

What do NDEs tell us about the meaning of life and death? 28

Chapter 5: The Life Review 30

What is the life review? 30

What do people see during their life reviews? 30

What is the purpose of the life review? 31

How can the life review help us to live better lives? 31

Chapter 6: Meeting Deceased Loved Ones 34

How common is meeting deceased loved ones during an NDE? 34

What do people say about their meetings with deceased loved ones? 34

What does meeting a deceased loved one during an NDE mean? 35

How can these experiences help us to cope with grief and loss? 36

Chapter 7: Religious and Spiritual Themes 38

What are the most common religious and spiritual themes associated with NDEs? 38

How do NDEs influence people's religious and spiritual beliefs? 39

What can we learn about God and the afterlife from NDEs? 40

How can NDEs help us to find meaning and purpose in our lives? 41

Chapter 8: Out-of-Body Experiences 43

What is an out-of-body experience (OBE)? 43

What do people experience during OBEs? 43

How can OBEs be explained by science? 44

What do OBEs tell us about the nature of consciousness? 45

Chapter 9: Tunnels and Lights 47

How common is seeing tunnels and lights during an NDE? 47

What do people say about their experiences with tunnels and lights? 47

What do tunnels and lights symbolize? 48

What do tunnels, and lights tell us about the transition from life to death? 49

Chapter 10: The Feeling of Unconditional Love 51

What is the feeling of unconditional love that many people experience during NDEs? 51

How does this feeling of love change people's lives? 52

What can we learn about the nature of love from NDEs? 52

How can we cultivate more love in our own lives? 53

Chapter 11: The Sense of Peace and Well-being 55

What is the feeling of peace and well-being many people experience during NDEs? 55

How does this feeling of peace change people's lives? . 56

What can we learn about the nature of peace and well-being from NDEs? 56

How can we cultivate more peace and well-being in our own lives? 57

Chapter 12: The Knowledge of the Future 59

How common is it to have knowledge of the future during an NDE? 59

What do people say about their experiences with knowledge of the future? 60

How can these experiences be explained? 60

What do they tell us about the nature of time and reality? 61

Chapter 13: The Return to Life 63

What happens when people return to life after an NDE? 63

What challenges do they face? 63

How do they adjust to life again? 64

What advice do they have for others who have had NDEs? 65

Chapter 14: The After Effects of NDEs 67

What are the long-term effects of NDEs on people's lives? 67

How do NDEs change people's values, beliefs, and priorities? 68

How do NDEs influence people's relationships with others? 68

How can people integrate their NDE experiences into their daily lives? 69

Chapter 15: NDEs from a Scientific Perspective 72

What do scientific studies tell us about NDEs? 72

What are the different theories about what causes NDEs? 73

What are the implications of NDE research for our understanding of consciousness and death? 74

Chapter 16: NDEs from a Religious Perspective 76
   How do different religions interpret NDEs? 76
   What do NDEs tell us about God and the afterlife?......77
   How can NDEs help us to strengthen our faith? 78

Chapter 17: NDEs from a Spiritual Perspective 80
   What do NDEs teach us about the nature of consciousness and reality?..80
   What do NDEs tell us about our place in the universe?81
   How can NDEs help us to live more meaningful and fulfilling lives?..82

Chapter 18: NDEs from a Cultural Perspective 84
   How do different culture view NDEs? 84
   How do NDEs influence people's cultural beliefs and practices?..85
   What can we learn about different cultures from their NDE stories?..86

Chapter 19: NDEs from a Personal Perspective.............88
   What it's like to have an NDE?......................................88
   How does an NDE change a person's life?...................89
   What advice do NDE experiencers have for others?.....90

Chapter 20: The Future of NDE Research 92
   What are the new directions in NDE research?............92
   What are the implications of NDE research for our understanding of life and death? 93
   How can NDE research help us to create a better future for humanity? 94

Chapter 21: NDEs and the Medical Community............97

How are NDEs perceived by the medical community? .97

What are the challenges of studying NDEs scientifically? 98

What new research methods are being developed to study NDEs? 99

What are the implications of NDE research for medical practice? 100

Chapter 22: NDEs and the Religious Community 103

How do different religions view NDEs? 103

How have NDEs influenced religious beliefs and practices throughout history? 104

What roles do NDEs play in contemporary religious communities? 105

How can NDEs help to bridge the gap between different religions? 106

Chapter 23: NDEs and the Media 109

How have NDEs been portrayed in the media? 109

What impact has the media had on public awareness of NDEs? 110

What are the challenges and opportunities of presenting NDEs accurately and respectfully in the media? 111

How can the media help to promote a deeper understanding of NDEs? 113

Chapter 25: NDEs and Popular Culture 115

How have NDEs been portrayed in popular culture, such as movies, TV shows, books, and music? 115

What impact has popular culture had on public understanding of NDEs? 116

What are the challenges and opportunities of presenting NDEs accurately and respectfully in popular culture?117

How can popular culture help to promote a deeper understanding of NDEs?......................................119

Chapter 26: NDEs and the Nature of Consciousness ..121

What do NDEs teach us about the nature of consciousness?..121

Is consciousness independent of the brain?..............121

Can consciousness survive the death of the body?....122

What are the implications of NDEs for our understanding of ourselves and our place in the universe? 123

Chapter 27: NDEs and the Afterlife............................125

What do NDEs tell us about the afterlife?..................125

Is there life after death? 126

What is the nature of the afterlife?............................126

What are the implications of NDEs for our understanding of death and dying?..........................127

Chapter 28: NDEs and the Meaning of Life.................130

What do NDEs teach us about the meaning of life?...130

Why are we here?...131

What is our purpose in life?.......................................131

How can we live more meaningful and fulfilling lives?132

Chapter 29: NDEs and the Future of Humanity...........134

What do NDEs teach us about the future of humanity? 134

Are we on the right track? 134

What can we do to create a better future for ourselves and future generations? 135

How can NDEs help us to become a more compassionate and loving species? 136

Chapter 30: Resources and Further Reading 140

Books That Illuminate the Afterlife: 140

Online Resources: 141

Communities of Support and Sharing: 142

Conclusion 144

Preface: In the Footsteps of Inspiration

There are moments when we find ourselves standing on the threshold of the unknown, staring into the abyss that separates the material world from the mysteries beyond. In these profound moments, we face the enigma of Near-Death Experiences (NDEs), a realm that beckons us to explore the uncharted territories of existence.

As we embark on this extraordinary journey into the heart of NDEs, it is only fitting to acknowledge the profound influence and inspiration that the work of Raymond Moody has had on this exploration. Dr. Moody's groundbreaking book, "Life After Life," first published in 1975, served as a beacon of light in NDE research. His pioneering efforts in documenting and analyzing NDEs laid the foundation for my quest to delve deeper into the subject.

Dr. Moody's work, filled with empathy, compassion, and a profound curiosity, has touched the hearts and minds of countless individuals, leading them to question the boundaries of life and death. His meticulous research and ability to convey the profoundly transformative nature of NDEs have inspired me and played an instrumental role in fostering an ever-growing interest in this captivating field of study.

In "Life After Life," Dr. Moody opened a door into the world of NDEs, inviting us to peer beyond the veil of the ordinary and into the extraordinary. His book catalyzed countless discussions, inquiries, and personal revelations. It paved the way for further research, fostering a global conversation about the profound implications of NDEs on our understanding of consciousness, spirituality, and the very essence of our existence.

As we journey through the pages of this book, we do so with the awareness that we stand on the shoulders of giants like Dr. Raymond Moody. I am inspired by his dedication to unraveling the mysteries of NDEs.

My aim in "Awakening to the Afterlife" is to build upon the foundation laid by Dr. Moody and countless other dedicated researchers, experiencers, and seekers of truth. I invite you to join me on this profound expedition as we navigate the terrain of the miraculous and the mystical, seeking to unravel the deep truths that NDEs hold.

As we embark upon this journey, the collective spirit of inquiry and wonder propels us forward. Together, we will explore the realms that defy easy explanation and endeavor to glimpse the profound mysteries that lie beyond the threshold of life and death.

Introduction:

It exists in a realm that transcends the boundaries of both science and spirituality. It beckons to us, enticing our curiosity and beckoning us to explore the profound mysteries that dwell within the very essence of existence. This mysterious terrain is none other than the enigma of Near-Death Experiences (NDEs).

What is a near-death experience (NDE)?

A near-death experience, or NDE, is a phenomenon that has long held humanity in awe and wonder. It is that rare yet profoundly captivating moment when an individual stands on the precipice between life and death and, in doing so, touches something extraordinary. It is an ethereal interlude where the line separating the physical from the metaphysical becomes blurred, offering a breathtaking glimpse into a world that defies our understanding.

How common are NDEs?

NDEs are not mere tales spun from the fabric of imagination; they are, in truth, more prevalent than one might ever imagine. People from diverse backgrounds, regardless of age, culture, or faith, have shared their accounts of these extraordinary events. NDEs unfold in the hushed rooms of hospitals, on the brink of catastrophic accidents, amidst the sterile environs of surgical theaters, and during the harrowing throes of life-threatening illnesses. NDEs are a universal phenomenon, transcending the confines of race, creed, and belief.

What are the different types of NDEs?

The exploration of NDEs reveals a tapestry woven in various hues and forms. Some recount the classic NDE, where they find themselves suspended above their lifeless bodies, bathed in an ethereal light of indescribable beauty. Others speak of encounters with departed loved ones or profound feelings of love and interconnectedness. Some describe their passage through mysterious tunnels and encounters with celestial beings. These myriad experiences paint a rich and multifaceted portrait of the NDE phenomenon.

What are the most common elements of NDEs?

While NDEs manifest in diverse forms, certain shared elements have emerged as recurring motifs. The sensation of departing one's physical condition, traversing a luminous tunnel, encountering departed relatives or spiritual entities, and experiencing an overwhelming sense of tranquility and love are among the defining characteristics of these experiences. These shared aspects beckon us to ponder: Could there be a realm of collective consciousness that surpasses our earthly comprehension?

Why are NDEs important?

The significance of NDEs extends far beyond individual narratives. These experiences challenge the fabric of our scientific knowledge and compel us to reconsider our perception of reality. They challenge the age-old dichotomy between science and spirituality, beckoning us to explore uncharted realms of human consciousness and the mysteries surrounding existence. NDEs are not mere anomalies; they serve as windows into the profound and the unknowable, inviting us to reassess our comprehension of life, death, and the core of our existence.

Within the pages of this book, we embark on a captivating journey into the heart of NDEs, traversing the realms of science and spirituality alike, as well as the seen and unseen. We delve into research, first-hand accounts and the enigmas enshrouding these experiences, all in our quest to unravel the profound truths they contain.

"Awakening to the Afterlife" shall guide this awe-inspiring voyage as we strive to unveil the concealed dimensions of existence that NDEs offer us. Join me on this exploration as we navigate the domains of the miraculous and the mystical, seeking answers that have intrigued humanity for countless generations.

Chapter 2: The Science of NDEs

What does brain science tell us about NDEs?

In our quest to unravel the profound mysteries of Near-Death Experiences (NDEs), we must turn our gaze toward the realm of brain science, for it is here that we find both intriguing insights and compelling questions. The human brain, a complex and intricate organ, has long been the focal point of our attempts to comprehend the enigma of NDEs.

Dr. Sam Parnia, a leading researcher in the field of NDEs, offers a thought-provoking perspective: "NDEs, by their very nature, challenge our understanding of the relationship between the brain and consciousness. They force us to question the conventional notion that consciousness is solely a product of brain activity."

Indeed, NDEs often occur when the brain is severely compromised, such as during cardiac arrest or trauma. According to conventional medical wisdom, such circumstances should render conscious experiences impossible. However, the accounts of NDE experiencers paint a different picture.

Take, for example, the story of Sarah, a cardiac arrest survivor who vividly recalls her NDE: "I felt myself leaving my body, rising above the chaos in the emergency room. I saw the doctors and nurses working on me from above. It was so real, as though I had a heightened sense of awareness. But my brain should have been offline at that moment."

Such experiences challenge the conventional understanding of brain function and consciousness. They beckon us to explore the possibility that consciousness may exist independently of the brain, or at the very least, that the relationship between the two is far more complex than we once thought.

Can NDEs be explained by hallucinations or other medical conditions?

Skeptics have often suggested that NDEs could be mere hallucinations resulting from a brain struggling to cope with the stress of a life-threatening situation. While it is true that some aspects of NDEs may bear a resemblance to hallucinatory experiences, the comprehensive nature of these encounters sets them apart.

Dr. Bruce Greyson, a psychiatrist renowned for his work on NDEs, counters this argument: "Hallucinations are typically chaotic and fragmented, often resembling random dream-like sequences. In contrast, NDEs are often described as highly organized, with clear narratives, vivid sensations, and a profound sense of meaning."

Furthermore, the experiences of blind individuals who report NDEs pose a particularly compelling challenge to the hallucination hypothesis. How could individuals blind from birth describe visual details consistent with their NDEs if these were mere products of their imagination?

Consider the account of Michael, blind from birth, who described his NDE: "I could see colors and shapes, something I had never experienced in my life. It was as though I had been given the gift of sight, even briefly."

Such testimonies force us to dig deeper into the true nature of NDEs, raising questions about the relationship between consciousness, the brain, and the possibility of an existence beyond the physical.

What are the implications of NDEs for our understanding of consciousness and death?

NDEs have profound implications that extend far beyond the boundaries of medical science. They challenge our preconceptions about consciousness and the ultimate mystery of death itself.

Dr. Eben Alexander, a neurosurgeon who underwent a life changing NDE, reflects: "My own experience shattered the conventional wisdom of my field. I was in a coma, my brain besieged by a rare illness, yet I had an NDE that defied all scientific explanation. It made me reevaluate everything I thought I knew about the brain and consciousness."

NDEs urge us to reconsider the nature of human consciousness, suggesting that it may not be confined to the biological confines of our brains. They inspire us to question whether death is merely the end of our physical existence or if it marks the beginning of a new journey, as countless NDE experiencers have attested.

As we delve deeper into the science of NDEs, we find ourselves at the precipice of a profound transformation in our understanding of the human experience. The tales of those who have ventured to the threshold of life and death challenge us to redefine the boundaries of consciousness, embrace the possibility of a reality beyond the physical, and approach the grand mystery of death with newfound awe and wonder.

Chapter 3: The Stories of NDEs

First-hand accounts of NDEs from people from all walks of life.

In exploring Near-Death Experiences (NDEs), we embark on a profound journey through the stories of those who have traversed the threshold of existence and returned with remarkable tales. These stories, recounted by individuals from diverse backgrounds and circumstances, provide us with a tapestry of experiences that transcend the boundaries of culture, religion, and social status.

Meet Jane, a schoolteacher from a small town who faced a life-threatening illness. She describes her NDE with heartfelt sincerity: "As I hovered above my body, I felt an overwhelming sense of peace and love. I saw a radiant light that seemed to beckon me, and I felt a profound connection to everything in the universe. It was a reality more real than anything I had ever known."

And then there's John, a combat veteran who found himself in the throes of a life-threatening situation on the battlefield. He recalls his NDE with awe and humility: "In that moment, I felt a presence, a divine light that enveloped me. I knew I was not alone, and a deep sense of purpose filled my heart. It changed the way I viewed life and death forever."

These stories remind us that NDEs are not confined to the pages of medical journals or the annals of scientific research. They are deeply personal experiences that touch the lives of ordinary people in extraordinary ways.

The impact of NDEs on people's lives

The impact of NDEs extends far beyond the momentary glimpse into the unknown. They often leave an indelible mark on the lives of those who have undergone them, transforming their perspectives and priorities.

Susan, a successful businesswoman, shares her post-NDE journey: "After my NDE, I found that material success held far less importance for me. Instead, I became more focused on cultivating meaningful relationships and acts of kindness. My NDE reshaped my priorities, leading me to live a more fulfilling life."

For many NDE experiencers, the profound sense of interconnectedness and love they encounter during their NDEs becomes a guiding principle. They often develop a heightened empathy and compassion for others, recognizing the inherent value of every soul.

The lessons that people have learned from their NDEs

NDEs offer valuable lessons that resonate not only with the experiencers themselves but also with the broader world. These lessons often transcend the confines of religious or cultural beliefs, speaking to a universal truth about the nature of human existence.

One recurring theme in NDEs is the importance of love and compassion. Mary, a mother who faced a life-threatening childbirth, explains, "During my NDE, I was shown that love is the fabric of the universe. Every act of kindness and love we share has a ripple effect that transcends our physical existence."

Another lesson from NDE accounts is that life is a precious gift. Many NDE survivors speak of a newfound appreciation for the beauty of everyday existence, no matter how mundane it may seem.

In the pages of these stories, we find inspiration and wisdom that challenge us to live with greater purpose, empathy, and gratitude. They beckon us to consider the profound possibility that NDEs are not mere glimpses into an afterlife but profound messages from the cosmos about the essence of our shared humanity. Through these stories, we are reminded that even in the face of death, there is light, love, and the potential for transformation that transcends our earthly existence.

Chapter 4: The Truth About NDEs

What can we learn from NDEs about the afterlife?

Near-death experiences (NDEs) beckon us to peer into the great unknown, sparking profound questions about the existence of an afterlife. The accounts of those who have journeyed to the threshold of life and death provide us with glimpses into a realm that transcends the boundaries of our physical world.

In the words of Dr. Raymond Moody, whose work laid the foundation for our understanding of NDEs, "NDEs offer a tantalizing glimpse into the possibility of an afterlife. The consistent themes of peace, love, and a radiant light suggest that consciousness may continue beyond the physical realm."

The experiences recounted by NDE survivors often describe a place of unparalleled beauty, where love and interconnectedness are pervasive. They speak of encounters with departed loved ones, celestial beings, and a sense of profound purpose. These narratives challenge us to reconsider the finality of death and open a doorway to the tantalizing possibility of an afterlife.

Do NDEs provide evidence for a soul or consciousness beyond the body?

One of the most compelling questions posed by NDEs revolves around the existence of a soul or consciousness that transcends the confines of the physical body. Dr. Eben Alexander, a neurosurgeon who underwent a transformative NDE, reflects on this profound question: "My experience shattered the conventional notion that consciousness is a mere product of brain activity. It pointed to the existence of a consciousness independent of the body."

NDEs' vivid and organized nature challenges the hypothesis that they are mere hallucinations or neurological glitches. Instead, they suggest that consciousness may exist as a separate entity, capable of functioning independently from the brain.

The stories of individuals who have encountered deceased relatives and communicated with them during their NDEs further fuel this intriguing possibility. They offer a tantalizing glimpse into the continuity of consciousness beyond death, inviting us to contemplate the profound implications for our understanding of life and its ultimate destination.

What do NDEs tell us about the meaning of life and death?

At the heart of NDEs lies a message that transcends religious, cultural, and philosophical boundaries. These experiences often reveal a profound sense of purpose and meaning in life and a deeper understanding of death.

As Mary, a hospice nurse who has accompanied many souls in their final moments, shares: "NDEs remind us that life is a gift, and every moment is precious. They encourage us to live with love and compassion, cherish our connections, and embrace the profound journey of self-discovery."

NDEs offer a unique perspective on death, suggesting that it is not the end but a transition to another state of existence. They impart the idea that death is not to be feared but embraced as a part of the grand tapestry of existence.

In the stories of NDE survivors, we find a powerful message about the profound interconnectedness of all living beings and the enduring nature of love and consciousness. They beckon us to contemplate the possibility that NDEs are windows to a reality beyond our comprehension, offering us glimpses of the profound truths that await us on the other side of life's mysterious threshold. Through NDEs, we are reminded that life and death are part of a grand and awe-inspiring journey that invites us to explore the boundless dimensions of our existence.

Chapter 5: The Life Review

What is the life review?

The life review, a remarkable aspect of many Near-Death Experiences (NDEs), is a profound journey into one's past. It is a moment of introspection and reflection, where individuals revisit the pivotal moments of their lives with unparalleled clarity and depth. During this extraordinary experience, individuals often watch their lives unfold like a vivid movie playing before their eyes.

What do people see during their life reviews?

People witness a panoramic view of their existence. They revisit their actions and the emotions, thoughts, and intentions that accompany them. Every interaction, no matter how small, takes on profound significance. An NDE experiencer, Susan, describes her life review: "I saw the ripple effects of my actions, how a small act of kindness or a harsh word could impact others in ways I had never fully grasped."

The life review isn't just a chronological playback of events; it is a visceral re-experiencing of the emotions and perspectives of each moment. People often describe feeling a deep empathy for others they have encountered, seeing situations from the viewpoint of those they had interacted with.

What is the purpose of the life review?

The life review serves as a profound learning opportunity. It allows individuals to gain insight into the consequences of their actions, fostering a deep understanding of their impact on others. This introspection often leads to a heightened sense of accountability and a desire for personal growth and positive change.

Dr. Kenneth Ring, a pioneer in NDE research, explains: "The life review is a powerful mechanism for self-reflection and transformation. It is an opportunity to recognize all beings' interconnectedness and embrace the profound lessons of empathy, love, and forgiveness."

How can the life review help us to live better lives?

The lessons gleaned from the life review are profound and far-reaching. Daily, they inspire individuals to strive for greater compassion, kindness, and understanding. NDE experiencers often return from their encounters with a renewed commitment to live more purposefully and authentically.

John, an NDE survivor, shares his perspective: "My life review made me acutely aware of the impact of my actions on others. It inspired me to mend broken relationships and prioritize love and connection above all else. It's a lesson I carry with me every day."

The life review, with its capacity to awaken empathy and promote self-improvement, underscores the transformative power of NDEs. It challenges us to consider the profound potential for personal growth and positive change these experiences offer to those who have undergone them and society.

As we delve into the intricate tapestry of the life review, we uncover a timeless lesson about the significance of our actions and the enduring power of love and compassion. Through the stories of NDE survivors, we are reminded that every moment holds the potential for profound impact and every choice we make ripples through our existence. In the life review, we find a powerful call to live with greater intention, to nurture our connections with others, and to embrace the transformative journey of self-discovery.

Chapter 6: Meeting Deceased Loved Ones

How common is meeting deceased loved ones during an NDE?

Among the myriad facets of Near-Death Experiences (NDEs), the encounters with deceased loved ones are a particularly poignant and heartwarming theme. These reunions offer a glimpse into the enduring nature of human connections beyond the threshold of life and death. It is a common thread that weaves through many NDE accounts, transcending cultural, religious, and geographic boundaries.

What do people say about their meetings with deceased loved ones?

NDE experiencers who encounter deceased loved ones often describe these encounters with profound emotion and vivid detail. They speak of being enveloped in an overwhelming sense of love and joy as if they were reunited with a part of their essence.

Mark, who had a life-threatening accident, shares his experience: "I saw my grandmother, who had passed away years ago. She looked as radiant and loving as I remembered her from my childhood. It was as if all the pain and suffering I had endured vanished in her presence."

These accounts frequently describe conversations or exchanges of messages that convey a deep sense of comfort and reassurance. Loved ones often say it is not their time to join them, encouraging the experience to return to life with renewed purpose.

What does meeting a deceased loved one during an NDE mean?

The encounters with deceased loved ones during NDEs hold profound significance. They challenge conventional notions of death as a final and irrevocable separation. Instead, these experiences suggest that our connections with those we cherish endure beyond the grave, offering a glimmer of hope and solace to those who grieve.

Dr. Raymond Moody, whose pioneering work first brought attention to the phenomenon of NDEs, reflects: "Meeting deceased loved ones during NDEs speaks to the enduring power of love and the interconnectedness of all souls. It invites us to reconsider the nature of our existence and the bonds that transcend the physical world."

How can these experiences help us to cope with grief and loss?

NDEs that involve encounters with deceased loved ones offer a unique form of healing and solace to those who grapple with grief and loss. These experiences often provide a profound sense of closure, as individuals are reassured that their loved ones are at peace and continue to watch over them.

Jane, who lost her son to a tragic accident, shares her experience: "During my NDE, I was reunited. He told me he was okay, still loved me, and would always be with me. It brought me immeasurable comfort and helped me find a way to move forward."

These encounters can be transformative, offering a sense of purpose and renewed hope to those who have experienced loss. They serve as a testament to the enduring bonds of love and connection that transcend the boundaries of life and death, and they remind us that even in our darkest moments, there is the potential for healing, growth, and profound transformation.

In the stories of NDE survivors who have encountered their deceased loved ones, we find a powerful reminder that love is an eternal force that transcends the confines of time and space. Through these experiences, we are offered a glimpse into the profound mysteries of existence and the enduring nature of the human spirit. They invite us to consider that our connections with those we cherish remain unbroken even in death, offering solace and hope amid our deepest sorrows.

Chapter 7: Religious and Spiritual Themes

What are the most common religious and spiritual themes associated with NDEs?

Near-death experiences (NDEs) often serve as profound conduits for religious and spiritual themes, offering glimpses into realms that transcend our earthly understanding. These themes, though diverse, reveal striking commonalities that bridge cultural and religious divides.

One of the most prevalent themes is encountering a radiant, all-encompassing light often described as divine. This light represents an overwhelming sense of love, peace, and unity, inviting comparisons to the concept of God or a higher power in various religious traditions.

Angelic beings or spiritual guides frequently appear in NDEs, providing comfort, guidance, and a sense of purpose. These entities are often perceived as messengers from the divine, guiding the experience toward a deeper understanding of their spiritual journey.

Many NDE accounts also feature a life review, wherein individuals witness their past actions and impact on others. This theme resonates with karma, or the moral consequences of one's actions, in various religious and philosophical traditions.

How do NDEs influence people's religious and spiritual beliefs?

NDEs profoundly influence individuals' religious and spiritual beliefs, often leading to transformative shifts in their perspectives. These experiences challenge conventional religious dogma and encourage a more personal and inclusive spirituality.

Dr. Kenneth Ring, a leading researcher in NDE studies, notes: "NDEs often lead individuals to embrace a more universal and less dogmatic spirituality. They tend to emphasize the importance of love, compassion, and interconnectedness as core spiritual values."

Many NDE experiencers report feeling less attached to religious doctrines and more drawn to the essence of their faith, seeking a deeper, more personal connection with the divine. These encounters can spark a profound sense of spirituality that transcends traditional religious boundaries, fostering a sense of unity with all of humanity.

What can we learn about God and the afterlife from NDEs?

NDEs provide tantalizing glimpses into the nature of God and the afterlife, offering perspectives that challenge and enrich our understanding of these profound concepts. Experiencers often describe the divine as an all-encompassing, unconditional love, a presence that transcends human comprehension.

Sarah, who had an NDE, reflects: "I encountered a light so radiant and loving that it felt like home. It was a presence that knew me intimately and accepted me unconditionally. It redefined my understanding of God as pure love."

These encounters with the divine suggest that God is not a distant, judgmental figure but a source of boundless compassion and understanding. They invite us to reconsider our relationship with the Holy and the potential for a more profound, personal connection.

How can NDEs help us to find meaning and purpose in our lives?

NDEs can instill a profound sense of meaning and purpose in those who undergo them. The encounter with the divine, the life review, and the lessons learned during NDEs often inspire individuals to live with greater intention and authenticity.

NDE experiencers frequently return with a heightened awareness of the importance of love, compassion, and empathy. They prioritize relationships and acts of kindness, recognizing that these are the true treasures of existence.

John, an NDE survivor, expresses the transformative impact of his experience: "My NDE made me realize that life is about love, connection, and the way we treat others. It has given me a sense of purpose to be a source of love and kindness."

These profound lessons remind us that life's meaning and purpose are not elusive concepts but are found in the simple acts of love and connection that define our shared human experience. NDEs beckon us to consider that our spiritual journey is intimately tied to our capacity to love and to find meaning in every moment of existence.

In exploring NDEs' religious and spiritual themes, we find a profound tapestry of experiences that transcends religious boundaries and fosters a more inclusive, compassionate spirituality. Through these encounters with the divine, we are reminded that love is at the heart of our spiritual journey and that our actions in this world can have a profound impact on our lives and the lives of others. NDEs challenge us to embrace a spirituality rooted in love, empathy, and interconnectedness, inviting us to live with greater purpose and authenticity.

Chapter 8: Out-of-Body Experiences

What is an out-of-body experience (OBE)?

Out-of-body experiences (OBEs) are among the most captivating and enigmatic phenomena. During an OBE, individuals report a sensation of detaching from their physical bodies, often floating above or beside themselves, while maintaining their consciousness and awareness.

These experiences have been documented across diverse cultures and periods, transcending boundaries of belief and skepticism. They offer a profound lens through which we can explore the nature of human consciousness and the mysteries of existence.

What do people experience during OBEs?

The accounts of those who have undergone OBEs reveal a remarkable array of sensations and perceptions. People describe feeling weightless, as though they are effortlessly gliding or floating above their physical bodies. They often report a heightened sense of clarity and awareness, as if seeing the world from a new vantage point.

The ability to move through physical barriers, such as walls or ceilings, is a common theme in OBEs. Individuals recount journeys through their homes or hospital rooms, providing details that would be impossible to perceive from their physical location.

Moreover, many OBE experiencers describe encounters with deceased loved ones, spiritual beings, or otherworldly realms. These encounters often evoke powerful emotions, ranging from profound peace and joy to awe and wonder.

How can OBEs be explained by science?

The scientific explanation for OBEs remains a subject of ongoing research and debate. Some theories suggest that OBEs may be related to altered brain states, such as during sleep paralysis or near-sleep experiences. These altered states could disrupt the brain's usual sense of body awareness, leading to the perception of an OBE.

Others propose that OBEs might be linked to specific brain regions, such as the temporoparietal junction, crucial in processing sensory information and body awareness. Disruptions or malfunctions in this region could trigger OBE-like experiences.

However, these scientific explanations need to fully account for the rich and vivid nature of OBEs, which often involve detailed perceptions of the external environment and encounters with entities or beings. The precise mechanisms underlying OBEs continue to elude our understanding, raising questions about the relationship between consciousness and the physical body.

What do OBEs tell us about the nature of consciousness?

OBEs offer a tantalizing glimpse into the profound mystery of consciousness. These experiences challenge our conventional understanding of the relationship between consciousness and the physical body, suggesting that consciousness may exist independently of the brain.

Dr. Bruce Greyson, a psychiatrist and researcher of OBEs, reflects: "OBEs force us to reconsider the nature of consciousness and its connection to the body. They hint at the possibility that consciousness is not confined to the brain but can exist as a separate, non-localized phenomenon."

The accounts of individuals who have undergone OBEs paint a picture of consciousness as a dynamic and multifaceted aspect of human existence. They beckon us to explore the nature of our awareness and the possibility that it may extend beyond the boundaries of our physical selves.

Through the lens of OBEs, we are invited to delve into the profound mysteries of consciousness, the nature of reality, and our place in the universe. These experiences challenge us to embrace the enigma of human existence and consider consciousness's limitless potential. In doing so, they inspire us to embark on a journey of discovery that transcends the confines of our physical bodies and opens the door to the boundless realms of the mind and spirit.

Chapter 9: Tunnels and Lights

How common is seeing tunnels and lights during an NDE?

In Near-Death Experiences (NDEs), the appearance of tunnels and radiant lights is a recurrent and compelling theme. It is a phenomenon that transcends cultural, religious, and geographic boundaries, occurring in the accounts of NDE experiencers from all walks of life.

These encounters with tunnels and lights during NDEs evoke a sense of wonder and curiosity, drawing us into the mysteries that lie beyond the threshold of life and death.

What do people say about their experiences with tunnels and lights?

Individuals who have undergone NDEs often describe the sensation of traveling through a tunnel toward a radiant light. The tunnel is typically depicted as a passageway that envelops them, guiding them away from their physical surroundings. An overwhelming sense of peace, love, and tranquility marks this journey.

Mark, who had an NDE after a life-threatening accident, shares his experience: "I found myself in a tunnel, surrounded by a warm, inviting light. It was like I was being gently drawn toward something greater than myself. The love and comfort I felt were beyond words."

The radiant light encountered in NDEs is often described as intensely bright, yet it doesn't cause discomfort or pain to the experiencer. Instead, it radiates a profound sense of love, acceptance, and warmth, as if it embodies divine or transcendent energy.

What do tunnels and lights symbolize?

Tunnels and lights in NDEs symbolize the journey from the known to the unknown, from the physical to the spiritual. They represent a transition between life as we know it and the mysteries of the afterlife or the greater cosmos.

These symbols often serve as a guiding force, leading individuals toward a profound encounter with the divine or a heightened state of awareness. The tunnel can be seen as a bridge between the earthly and spiritual realms, offering a path of transformation and transcendence.

Moreover, the radiant light is frequently interpreted as a manifestation of love and enlightenment. It symbolizes the ultimate source of all creation, a presence that radiates boundless compassion and understanding.

What do tunnels, and lights tell us about the transition from life to death?

Tunnels and lights during NDEs offer profound insights into the transition from life to death. They suggest this transition is not a journey into darkness or emptiness but a passage toward a luminous, loving, and transformative experience.

Dr. Raymond Moody reflects: "Tunnels and lights in NDEs speak to the universal themes of transformation and transcendence. They hint at the idea that death is not an end but a transition to a state of existence filled with love and meaning."

These symbols remind us that the transition from life to death is a natural part of our existence that can be embraced with hope and awe. They invite us to consider that, even in the face of death, a radiant light beckon us, a light that embodies love, acceptance, and the promise of a journey into the infinite.

Through the experiences of tunnels and lights in NDEs, we are offered a profound message about the nature of our existence and the continuity of consciousness beyond the physical realm. They inspire us to approach the mystery of life and death with wonder and reverence, reminding us that even in our final moments, there is the potential for transcendence and illumination.

Chapter 10: The Feeling of Unconditional Love

What is the feeling of unconditional love that many people experience during NDEs?

One of the most profound and transformative aspects of Near-Death Experiences (NDEs) is the overwhelming sensation of unconditional love that envelops those who undergo these extraordinary journeys. This love transcends human understanding, offering a glimpse into boundless compassion, acceptance, and interconnectedness.

During NDEs, individuals often encounter a radiant light or presence that emanates this love. It surrounds them, infusing them with a profound sense of warmth, peace, and acceptance. It is a love that knows no judgment, conditions, or limitations and is as boundless as the universe.

How does this feeling of love change people's lives?

The experience of unconditional love during an NDE often leaves an indelible mark on the lives of those who have undergone it. It is a love transcends the boundaries of ego and self-interest, inspiring individuals to live with greater compassion, empathy, and authenticity.

Susan, an NDE experiencer, shared: "After my NDE, I carried that feeling of love with me every day. It changed how I interacted with others, fostering deeper connections and kindness. I felt a profound sense of purpose to be a source of love."

Many NDE survivors report a heightened sense of empathy, a deepened capacity for forgiveness, and a greater appreciation for the beauty and interconnectedness of all life. The love they encounter during their NDEs becomes a guiding principle, reshaping their priorities and inspiring them to seek meaningful, loving connections.

What can we learn about the nature of love from NDEs?

NDEs offer a profound lesson about the nature of love—that it is the essence of our existence, the fundamental fabric of the universe itself. The love experienced during NDEs is not conditional upon external factors or personal worthiness; it is a love that flows unconditionally, embracing all beings without exception.

Dr. Kenneth Ring, a researcher in NDEs, reflects: "NDEs reveal that love is the most powerful force in the universe. It is the foundation of our existence, the source of all meaning and purpose. It is a force that transcends time and space, binding all creation together."

Through the lens of NDEs, we are invited to contemplate that love is not merely an emotion but a universal, spiritual truth. It is a force that connects us all, uniting the threads of our individual lives into a magnificent tapestry of existence.

How can we cultivate more love in our own lives?

The lessons of NDEs offer a profound blueprint for cultivating more love in our lives. We can begin by recognizing every individual's inherent worth and dignity, practicing empathy and understanding, and embracing forgiveness and compassion as guiding principles.

By nurturing our connections with others, seeking to understand their experiences and perspectives, and offering kindness and support, we can cultivate love in our daily interactions. We can strive to live authentically, aligning our actions with our values and priorities and becoming vessels of love in the world.

Moreover, we can engage in practices that foster inner peace and self-love, such as meditation, gratitude, and self-reflection. We become better equipped to share love and kindness with others by tending to our well-being.

In the radiant love experienced during NDEs, we find a profound reminder that love is not merely an emotion but the essence of our existence. Through these experiences, we are challenged to embrace a life guided by love, compassion, and empathy, to recognize the interconnectedness of all living beings, and to seek the transformative power of love in every moment of our existence. In doing so, we honor the profound message of NDEs—that love is the ultimate force of healing and transformation in our lives and the world.

Chapter 11: The Sense of Peace and Well-being

What is the feeling of peace and well-being many people experience during NDEs?

In the profound tapestry of Near-Death Experiences (NDEs), the overwhelming sensation of peace and well-being is a constant and transcendent theme. Those who undergo NDEs often describe this profound feeling as the essence of their encounters—a sense of serenity, contentment, and tranquility that transcends human comprehension.

During NDEs, individuals often find themselves immersed in profound peace and well-being. It is a peace that transcends the chaos of the physical world, a well-being that emanates from a deeper, spiritual source. It is a peace that knows no fear, suffering, and limitations—a well-being that is as boundless as the cosmos.

How does this feeling of peace change people's lives?

The experience of peace and well-being during an NDE has a profound and lasting impact on the lives of those who have undergone it. It catalyzes personal transformation, inspiring individuals to seek inner peace and well-being daily.

An NDE experiencer, Mary, shares her transformation: "The peace I encountered during my NDE became my guiding light. It changed how I approached life's challenges, helping me find serenity even amid chaos. It was a gift that reshaped my priorities."

NDE survivors often return with a renewed inner calm, resilience, and acceptance. They are better equipped to navigate life's trials and tribulations as they carry the memory of the profound peace they encountered during their journeys.

What can we learn about the nature of peace and well-being from NDEs?

NDEs offer a profound lesson about the nature of peace and well-being—that they are not contingent upon external circumstances but are innate aspects of our spiritual essence. The peace experienced during NDEs reflects the soul's true nature, a state of being that exists beyond the physical world's limitations.

Dr. Raymond Moody, a pioneering researcher in NDEs, reflects: "NDEs reveal that peace and well-being are not elusive goals but inherent aspects of our existence. They are the birthright of every soul, a reflection of our interconnectedness with the cosmos."

Through the lens of NDEs, we are invited to consider that peace and well-being are not fleeting or conditional but are states of being that can be cultivated and embraced in our daily lives. They are the keys to a life with greater authenticity, resilience, and inner harmony.

How can we cultivate more peace and well-being in our own lives?

The lessons of NDEs provide a profound roadmap for cultivating more peace and well-being in our lives. We can begin by practicing mindfulness, self-compassion, and gratitude, which can help us connect with our inner sense of peace.

Engaging in relaxation techniques, meditation, and time in nature can also nurture our inner well-being. By promoting our physical, emotional, and spiritual health, we can create a foundation for lasting peace.

Moreover, embracing purpose and service to others can infuse our lives with a more profound sense of meaning and contentment. Kindness, compassion, and generosity can lead to a sense of well-being that transcends personal concerns and extends to the greater community.

In the profound peace and well-being experienced during NDEs, we find a timeless message—that these states of being are not distant or unattainable but are inherent aspects of our spiritual nature. Through these experiences, we are challenged to embrace a life guided by inner peace and well-being, to recognize the interconnectedness of all living beings, and to seek the transformative power of peace in every moment of our existence. In doing so, we honor the profound message of NDEs—that peace is the ultimate source of healing and transformation in our lives and the world.

Chapter 12: The Knowledge of the Future

How common is it to have knowledge of the future during an NDE?

Within the intricate tapestry of Near-Death Experiences (NDEs), glimpses of future knowledge stand as a captivating and intriguing theme. While not as prevalent as other elements of NDEs, such as encounters with deceased loved ones or feelings of peace and love, the knowledge of the future does occur in the accounts of some NDE experiencers.

These glimpses into the future challenge our conventional understanding of time and reality, offering a tantalizing hint of the mysteries that lie beyond our earthly existence.

What do people say about their experiences with knowledge of the future?

NDE survivors who have glimpsed the future often recount a profound sense of clarity and certainty about events yet to unfold. These glimpses are typically brief and vivid, providing details later confirmed as accurate.

Sarah, who had an NDE after a car accident, shares her experience: "During my NDE, I saw myself in a hospital room, surrounded by loved ones. It felt so real. Months later, I found myself in that exact scenario. It was as if I had already lived it."

The knowledge of the future in NDEs is often marked by a deep understanding and acceptance of the events to come. It is not characterized by fear or anxiety but by a serene recognition of the unfolding of life's mysteries.

How can these experiences be explained?

The phenomenon of knowledge of the future during NDEs remains a subject of both wonder and scientific inquiry. Some theories suggest that these glimpses may be related to altered states of consciousness, wherein individuals access information beyond the constraints of linear time.

In the realm of quantum physics, the concept of non-locality hints at the interconnectedness of all particles in the universe, suggesting that information may not be bound by the limitations of space and time. Some speculate that NDEs offer a temporary opening of awareness to this interconnected web of existence, enabling individuals to perceive events yet to occur.

Yet, these explanations remain speculative, and the precise mechanisms underlying knowledge of the future during NDEs continue to elude our understanding.

What do they tell us about the nature of time and reality?

The glimpses of future knowledge in NDEs make us reconsider the nature of time and reality. Our conventional understanding of time as a linear, unidirectional flow may need to be completed.

Dr. Bruce Greyson, a researcher in NDE studies, reflects: "NDEs challenge us to consider that time may be more fluid and interconnected than we once believed. They hint at the idea that our consciousness may transcend the constraints of linear time, offering glimpses into the future as well as the past."

These experiences remind us that our understanding of reality is far more complex and mysterious than we can fathom. They invite us to consider that our perception of time and the boundaries of reality may be constructs of our earthly existence, concealing deeper truths that lie beyond our current comprehension.

In the knowledge of the future glimpsed during NDEs, we are offered a tantalizing clue that the mysteries of time and reality are yet to be fully unraveled. These experiences challenge us to embrace a sense of wonder and humility in the face of existence's profound enigmas, beckoning us to explore the boundless depths of the human spirit and the universe.

Chapter 13: The Return to Life

What happens when people return to life after an NDE?

Returning to life following a Near-Death Experience (NDE) is a profound and often transformative journey. After encountering the mysteries of the afterlife or otherworldly realms, NDE survivors must grapple with the challenge of reintegrating into the earthly realm, where the ordinary and extraordinary coexist.

For many, the transition is marked by disorientation as they return to their physical bodies. They may initially struggle to reconcile their NDEs' vivid memories with the material world's constraints. Yet, this return also promises a deeper understanding of life's purpose and a newfound appreciation for the preciousness of existence.

What challenges do they face?

NDE survivors often face a unique set of challenges upon their return to life. They may grapple with the profound nature of their experiences, which can be challenging to convey to others who have not undergone NDEs. The fear of being misunderstood or met with skepticism can be isolating.

Moreover, some NDE experiencers find it challenging to reintegrate into their daily routines, as the insights gained during their NDEs may lead them to question the priorities and values of mainstream society. They may struggle to find meaning and purpose in their lives, longing to align their actions with the lessons learned during their NDEs.

Reacclimatizing the physical world can be emotionally taxing as individuals strive to balance the transcendental insights gained during their NDEs with the practical demands of everyday life.

How do they adjust to life again?

Adjusting to life again after an NDE is a multifaceted and deeply personal process. Many NDE survivors find solace in connecting with support groups or therapists specializing in NDE experiences. These interactions provide a safe space to share their stories and receive validation for their extraordinary encounters.

The integration process often involves exploring the lessons learned during the NDE and finding ways to apply them to daily life; this may include cultivating a more profound sense of compassion, nurturing meaningful relationships, and aligning one's actions with a greater sense of purpose.

Meditation and mindfulness practices can also help individuals ground themselves in the present moment and maintain a sense of inner peace as they navigate the challenges of the physical world. These practices enable NDE survivors to maintain a connection to the profound insights gained during their journeys.

What advice do they have for others who have had NDEs?

NDE survivors often offer valuable advice to others who have undergone similar experiences. They emphasize the importance of seeking support and understanding from those who have shared NDE journeys. Connecting with fellow experiencers can provide a sense of validation and a platform for sharing insights.

Furthermore, NDE survivors encourage those who have had NDEs to honor the transformative nature of their experiences. They suggest embracing the lessons learned during their NDEs and using them as a compass for living a more authentic and purposeful life.

An NDE survivor, Mark, reflects: "My advice to others who have had NDEs is to cherish the gift of life. Embrace the love, compassion, and insights gained during your journey, and let them guide you toward a life filled with meaning and connection."

In the return to life after an NDE, we find a testament to the resilience of the human spirit. NDE survivors remind us that, even after touching the realms beyond life, our existence here on Earth has a profound purpose. Their experiences offer hope and inspiration, encouraging us to seek more significant meaning, love, and authenticity.

Chapter 14: The After Effects of NDEs

What are the long-term effects of NDEs on people's lives?

The profound impact of Near-Death Experiences (NDEs) extends far beyond the moments of the actual encounters. These extraordinary journeys often bring about lasting and transformative effects on the lives of those who have undergone them.

Many NDE survivors report a heightened sense of inner peace, resilience, and acceptance that endures long after their experiences. They remember the unconditional love and boundless knowledge encountered during their NDEs, which continues to shape their perspectives and choices.

How do NDEs change people's values, beliefs, and priorities?

NDEs profoundly influence people's values, beliefs, and priorities. They often lead individuals to reevaluate their preconceived notions about life, death, and the nature of existence. Conventional beliefs and dogmas may be replaced by a more inclusive, spiritual perspective that transcends religious boundaries.

NDE experiencers frequently emphasize love, compassion, and empathy in their lives, recognizing these qualities as fundamental to their spiritual journey. Materialistic pursuits may lose their allure as individuals prioritize meaningful connections and acts of kindness over material possessions.

Moreover, NDE survivors often develop a more profound sense of purpose and meaning, seeking to align their actions with the lessons learned during their NDEs. They may become advocates for positive change, working to spread messages of love and transformation in their communities and beyond.

How do NDEs influence people's relationships with others?

NDEs profoundly influence people's relationships with others, fostering a more profound sense of connection and empathy. Many NDE survivors report a heightened ability to understand and empathize with the experiences of others, recognizing the interconnectedness of all living beings.

These experiences often lead to improved relationships with family and friends, as NDE survivors prioritize love, forgiveness, and compassion in their interactions. They may become more supportive and understanding partners, parents, and friends, seeking to nurture meaningful connections.

NDE survivors often feel a sense of duty to share the transformative insights gained during their journeys, inspiring others to embrace love and kindness in their own lives. They become conduits of healing and transformation, using their experiences to uplift and connect profoundly with others.

How can people integrate their NDE experiences into their daily lives?

Integrating NDE experiences into daily life is a deeply personal and ongoing journey. It often involves reflection, self-discovery, and a commitment to living aligned with the insights gained during the NDE.

NDE survivors may find solace in connecting with support groups or therapists specializing in NDE experiences. These interactions provide a safe and understanding space for processing the profound nature of their encounters.

Engaging in meditation, mindfulness, and gratitude can help individuals maintain a sense of inner peace and connection with the insights gained during their NDEs. These practices remind us of the boundless love and wisdom within us all.

Furthermore, NDE survivors often advocate for positive change in their communities and the world. They use their experiences as a catalyst for spreading messages of love, compassion, and transformation, seeking to create a more inclusive and compassionate world.

In the after-effects of NDEs, we witness the enduring power of these extraordinary journeys to reshape lives and perspectives. NDE survivors inspire us to seek more significant meaning, love, and authenticity in our lives, reminding us that even in the face of death, there is the potential for profound transformation and illumination.

Chapter 15: NDEs from a Scientific Perspective

What do scientific studies tell us about NDEs?

Scientific studies have delved into the fascinating realm of Near-Death Experiences (NDEs), shedding light on the nature and significance of these extraordinary phenomena. While NDEs are deeply personal and subjective experiences, research has provided valuable insights into common elements and patterns.

Many NDEs share striking similarities across diverse cultures and belief systems. These common elements include the sensation of leaving one's physical body, the experience of traveling through a tunnel or encountering a radiant light, and the overwhelming feeling of unconditional love and peace.

Neuroscientists and psychologists have employed various methods, including surveys and interviews with NDE survivors, to gather data on these experiences. Research findings have consistently demonstrated that NDEs have a profound and lasting impact on individuals, often leading to greater inner peace, empathy, and spiritual awareness.

What are the different theories about what causes NDEs?

The scientific community has put forth several theories to explain the occurrence of NDEs. One prominent theory suggests that NDEs may result from altered brain states during life-threatening situations, such as cardiac arrest or trauma. During these moments, the brain's oxygen and blood supply may be compromised, leading to unusual experiences and perceptions.

Another theory proposes that NDEs could be triggered by a surge of neurochemicals in the brain, such as endorphins or DMT (dimethyltryptamine). These substances, known for their hallucinogenic properties, may play a role in generating the vivid and mystical elements of NDEs.

However, these theories need to fully account for the depth and complexity of NDEs, as many experiencers report encountering accurate and verifiable information during their NDEs, such as details of events in distant locations or predictions of future events. These aspects challenge our current scientific understanding and invite further exploration.

What are the implications of NDE research for our understanding of consciousness and death?

NDE research carries profound implications for our understanding of consciousness and death. These experiences challenge conventional notions of consciousness as solely a product of brain activity, suggesting that consciousness may exist independently of the physical body.

Dr. Sam Parnia, a pioneer in NDE research, reflects: "NDEs force us to reconsider the nature of consciousness and its relationship to the body. They hint at the possibility that consciousness may continue beyond the point of clinical death, opening new frontiers in our understanding of the human mind."

Furthermore, NDEs offer insights into the nature of death itself. They present a compelling argument that death may not be the end of existence but rather a transition to a different state of consciousness or existence. This perspective challenges the prevailing fear and uncertainty surrounding death, offering hope and comfort to individuals grappling with mortality.

In pursuing scientific understanding, NDE research encourages us to approach these profound experiences with an open mind and a willingness to explore the mysteries beyond our current knowledge. It beckons us to consider that, in the realm of Near-Death Experiences, there may be keys to unraveling the enigmas of consciousness, death, and the ultimate nature of reality.

Chapter 16: NDEs from a Religious Perspective

How do different religions interpret NDEs?

Near-death experiences (NDEs) profoundly impact individuals' spiritual beliefs, transcending the boundaries of different religions and belief systems. While interpretations of NDEs can vary among religious traditions, there are common threads that resonate across many faiths.

In Christianity, some interpret NDEs as glimpses of the afterlife or encounters with Jesus Christ. NDE survivors often describe encounters with a loving, radiant presence, which aligns with Christian beliefs of divine love and forgiveness.

In Islam, NDEs may be seen as glimpses of the transition from earthly life to the hereafter. Accounts often mention encountering angels or a divine presence, reflecting

Islamic teachings about the afterlife and the presence of Allah.

In Hinduism, NDEs can be understood through the lens of reincarnation and the cycle of life and death. Some NDE survivors describe encounters with deities or beings of light, which resonate with Hindu concepts of divinity and the soul's journey.

Across various religious traditions, NDEs are often interpreted as spiritual awakenings or confirmations of the existence of a divine realm. While interpretations may differ, the underlying message of love, interconnectedness, and spiritual growth is a common theme that transcends religious boundaries.

What do NDEs tell us about God and the afterlife?

NDEs provide tantalizing glimpses into the nature of God and the afterlife, offering profound insights that resonate with the teachings of many religions. The encounters with a radiant light or divine presence during NDEs often lead experiencers to describe God as a being of unconditional love, acceptance, and compassion.

These experiences challenge the conventional human understanding of God as a distant or judgmental deity, inviting individuals to embrace a more intimate and personal relationship with the divine. NDE survivors often describe feeling unconditionally loved and accepted, reinforcing that love is at the heart of the divine nature.

Additionally, NDEs offer glimpses of an afterlife often portrayed as a realm of peace, beauty, and profound spiritual growth; this aligns with the teachings of many religions that describe the afterlife as a place of reward and spiritual evolution.

How can NDEs help us to strengthen our faith?

NDEs have the potential to strengthen and deepen one's faith, regardless of religious background. They provide experiential evidence of a divine and loving presence, affirming the beliefs of many religious traditions.

For individuals of faith, NDEs can serve as a powerful validation of their spiritual beliefs. They offer a tangible experience of divine love and acceptance, reinforcing that faith is not merely a set of doctrines but a lived experience of the sacred.

NDEs can also inspire individuals to reevaluate and deepen their faith. The encounters with the divine and the profound lessons learned during NDEs often lead individuals to seek a more meaningful and authentic expression of their faith. They may find themselves drawn to prayer, meditation, or acts of kindness as ways to nurture their spiritual connection.

Moreover, NDEs can promote interfaith understanding and tolerance by highlighting the common threads that run through different religious traditions. They remind us that, at their core, many religions share a message of love, compassion, and unity with the divine.

In Near-Death Experiences, individuals are challenged to explore the profound spiritual truths that resonate with their hearts and souls. NDEs offer a bridge between the earthly and the divine, inviting individuals to cultivate a deeper and more intimate relationship with God, embrace the mysteries of the afterlife, and strengthen their faith in the boundless power of love and spiritual growth.

Chapter 17: NDEs from a Spiritual Perspective

What do NDEs teach us about the nature of consciousness and reality?

Near-death experiences (NDEs) offer profound insights into the nature of consciousness and reality, transcending the boundaries of conventional understanding. These experiences challenge our perception of consciousness as a product of the brain, suggesting that consciousness may exist independently of the physical body.

NDE survivors often describe a sense of expanded awareness and heightened consciousness during their journeys. They may recount experiencing a life review where they relive past events with vivid clarity, suggesting that consciousness can transcend time and space constraints.

Furthermore, encounters with deceased loved ones or meetings with a radiant light presence challenge our understanding of reality as solely material and finite. NDEs hint at multidimensional realms beyond our earthly comprehension, inviting us to consider that consciousness may be a universal and interconnected force that transcends physical boundaries.

What do NDEs tell us about our place in the universe?

NDEs provide profound insights into our place in the universe, emphasizing our interconnectedness with all living beings and the cosmos. Experiencers often describe encounters with a radiant and all-encompassing love that transcends human understanding, reminding us that love is the foundation of our existence.

These experiences encourage a sense of unity and compassion, challenging our tendency to perceive ourselves as separate from others. NDE survivors often return with a deep appreciation for the interconnectedness of all life and a commitment to fostering love, empathy, and understanding in their interactions with others.

NDEs also invite us to reconsider our understanding of life and death. They suggest that death is not the end but a transition to another state of consciousness or existence. This perspective challenges the fear and uncertainty surrounding death, offering hope and reassurance about the continuity of life beyond the physical realm.

How can NDEs help us to live more meaningful and fulfilling lives?

NDEs hold the potential to guide us toward more meaningful and fulfilling lives by imparting profound lessons about the nature of existence. The overwhelming sensation of love and acceptance experienced during NDEs often becomes a guiding principle in the lives of survivors.

NDE survivors frequently prioritize love, compassion, and empathy in their interactions. They seek to nurture meaningful relationships and offer support and kindness to those around them. By doing so, they create a ripple effect of positive change in their communities and beyond.

Additionally, NDEs inspire individuals to live with greater authenticity and purpose. The lessons learned during these experiences often lead to reevaluating priorities, encouraging individuals to align their actions with their deepest values and aspirations.

NDEs also promote inner peace and resilience, enabling individuals to navigate challenges gracefully and equanimously. Practices such as meditation, mindfulness, and gratitude can help individuals maintain a connection to the profound insights gained during their NDEs, allowing them to live with more significant serenity and presence.

In Near-Death Experiences, individuals are offered a transformative journey that challenges conventional beliefs and perceptions. These experiences encourage us to explore the boundless depths of consciousness, embrace the interconnectedness of all life, and live with love, purpose, and authenticity. They remind us that, even in the face of life's mysteries, there is the potential for profound growth, understanding, and fulfillment.

Chapter 18: NDEs from a Cultural Perspective

How do different culture view NDEs?

Near-death experiences (NDEs) are a universal phenomenon that transcends cultural boundaries, but they are often perceived and interpreted in diverse ways across different cultures. Cultural beliefs and traditions shape the lens through which NDEs are understood and integrated into the fabric of society.

In some Western cultures, NDEs are often seen through a spiritual or religious lens. They are interpreted as glimpses of the afterlife or encounters with divine beings, aligning with Christian or Judeo-Christian beliefs of heaven and God's presence.

In many indigenous cultures, NDEs may be seen as a connection to the spirit world or a journey into the realm of ancestors. These experiences are often woven into the rich tapestry of cultural traditions, reinforcing that life and death are interconnected aspects of existence.

In Eastern cultures, NDEs may be viewed through the lens of reincarnation and karma. Some interpret these experiences as a glimpse into the cycle of birth, death, and rebirth, reflecting the beliefs of Hinduism and Buddhism.

How do NDEs influence people's cultural beliefs and practices?

NDEs profoundly influence people's cultural beliefs and practices, often challenging or expanding existing cultural frameworks. When individuals from diverse cultural backgrounds undergo NDEs, they may reinterpret their experiences within the context of their cultural traditions.

For some, NDEs reinforce existing cultural beliefs, providing experiential evidence of the afterlife or the existence of divine beings. These experiences may deepen individuals' commitment to their cultural practices and rituals as they seek to align their lives with the spiritual truths revealed during their NDEs.

On the other hand, NDEs can also lead to a broadening of cultural perspectives. Experiencers often become more open to diverse beliefs and traditions, recognizing the common thread of love, interconnectedness, and spiritual growth that runs through all cultures.

NDE survivors may find themselves drawn to practices from different cultures, such as meditation, mindfulness, or energy healing, as they seek to nurture their spiritual connection and integrate the lessons learned during their journeys.

What can we learn about different cultures from their NDE stories?

The stories of NDEs from different cultures offer a rich tapestry of human experience and belief systems. They remind us that, regardless of cultural background, there is a universal yearning for understanding the mysteries of life, death, and existence.

These stories also highlight the resilience and adaptability of cultural beliefs. NDEs challenge and expand these beliefs, inviting individuals to reinterpret their cultural narratives in light of their extraordinary experiences.

Moreover, the stories of NDEs from diverse cultures demonstrate the common human desire for love, connection, and spiritual growth. The overwhelming sensation of love and acceptance experienced during NDEs is a shared element that transcends cultural boundaries, emphasizing the universal nature of these profound experiences.

In Near-Death Experiences, we find a bridge connecting diverse cultures, belief systems, and traditions. These experiences encourage us to explore the rich tapestry of human spirituality and to appreciate the universal themes of love, interconnectedness, and transformation that unite us all, regardless of our cultural backgrounds.

Chapter 19: NDEs from a Personal Perspective

What it's like to have an NDE?

To have a Near-Death Experience (NDE) is to embark on a journey that defies easy description. It is a profound and intensely personal encounter with the mysteries of existence, often triggered by a life-threatening event. During an NDE, individuals may find themselves outside their physical bodies, witnessing their lifeless form or traveling through tunnels toward a radiant light of indescribable beauty.

The sensations experienced during an NDE are beyond the scope of ordinary human experience. Many report a sense of overwhelming peace, love, and acceptance as if they have returned to a place of ultimate belonging. Encounters with deceased loved ones or divine beings may occur, leaving an indelible mark on the soul.

Yet, NDEs are only sometimes uniformly blissful. Some individuals describe moments of fear or confusion, reflecting the complexity of these experiences. The common thread, however, is the profound sense that NDEs are more than mere hallucinations; they are encounters with a more profound reality that transcends the physical world.

How does an NDE change a person's life?

The impact of an NDE on a person's life is often profound and enduring. Survivors of NDEs return to their earthly existence with a heightened sense of purpose and perspective. The love and acceptance they encounter during their NDEs become guiding principles, leading to significant changes in their beliefs and priorities.

NDE experiencers often develop a deep appreciation for the interconnectedness of all life, nurturing meaningful relationships and becoming advocates for love, compassion, and empathy. They frequently place less importance on material possessions and societal expectations, focusing instead on stimulating their inner spiritual growth.

These experiences may also lead to a reevaluation of personal goals and ambitions. Individuals often seek to align their actions with the lessons learned during their NDEs, pursuing paths that promote love, understanding, and positive change in the world.

What advice do NDE experiencers have for others?

NDE experiencers offer valuable advice for those seeking to live more meaningful and authentic lives. They encourage individuals to embrace love, compassion, and empathy as guiding principles in their interactions with others. By doing so, they believe we can create a more compassionate and connected world.

Furthermore, NDE survivors emphasize the importance of nurturing meaningful relationships and cherishing the moments we share with loved ones. They remind us that life is a precious gift, and every interaction has the potential to be an opportunity for love and connection.

Many NDE experiencers advocate mindfulness and meditation as tools for maintaining a sense of inner peace and presence in daily life. These practices can help individuals align with the profound insights gained during their NDEs.

Above all, NDE survivors encourage us to live with authenticity and purpose. They remind us that we each have a unique journey filled with opportunities for growth and transformation. By embracing the lessons of love, compassion, and spiritual awareness, we can embark on a path that leads to a more meaningful and fulfilling life.

From the personal perspectives of NDE experiencers, we find a testament to the transformative power of these extraordinary journeys. Their stories inspire us to seek greater love, understanding, and authenticity in our lives, reminding us that even in the face of life's mysteries, there is the potential for profound growth, connection, and illumination.

Chapter 20: The Future of NDE Research

What are the new directions in NDE research?

The field of Near-Death Experience (NDE) research is evolving, driven by a growing curiosity to unravel the mysteries of these profound encounters. As technology and scientific understanding advance, new directions in NDE research are emerging.

Neuroscientific Exploration: Researchers are delving deeper into the neurological aspects of NDEs. Advanced brain imaging techniques and monitoring technology allow scientists to study the brain during NDEs, shedding light on the neural mechanisms behind these experiences.

Cross-Cultural Studies: There is a growing interest in conducting cross-cultural studies to explore how NDEs are perceived and interpreted in different cultural contexts. This approach helps us understand the universal and culture-specific aspects of NDEs.

Long-Term Effects: Researchers are increasingly focused on studying the long-term effects of NDEs on individuals' lives; this includes assessing the enduring impact of NDEs on mental health, relationships, and overall well-being.

Therapeutic Applications: NDE research explores these experiences' potential therapeutic applications. Some studies investigate how the insights gained during NDEs can be integrated into therapy to help individuals cope with trauma, anxiety, and end-of-life issues.

What are the implications of NDE research for our understanding of life and death?

NDE research carries profound implications for our understanding of life and death, challenging conventional beliefs and offering new perspectives.

The Nature of Consciousness: NDEs challenge the notion that consciousness is solely a product of the brain. They suggest that consciousness may exist independently of the physical body, opening up new frontiers in understanding the mind.

The Continuity of Life: NDEs imply that death may not be the end but a transition to another state of existence. This perspective offers hope and comfort to individuals grappling with mortality, fostering a more positive and peaceful view of death.

The Power of Love and Connection: NDEs consistently emphasize the importance of love, compassion, and interconnectedness. This insight encourages us to prioritize these qualities in our lives, fostering greater empathy and unity among humanity.

The Exploration of Multidimensional Realities: NDEs hint at multidimensional realms beyond our earthly comprehension; this challenges our limited understanding of reality and invites us to explore the mysteries that lie beyond.

How can NDE research help us to create a better future for humanity?

NDE research has the potential to contribute to a better future for humanity in several ways:

Fostering Compassion: The emphasis on love, empathy, and interconnectedness in NDEs can inspire individuals and societies to prioritize compassion and understanding, leading to a more harmonious and inclusive world.

Easing the Fear of Death: NDE research can help alleviate the fear of death by providing evidence of the continuation of consciousness beyond the physical body; this can lead to a more peaceful and accepting approach to the end of life.

Advancing Mental Health: Insights gained from NDE research may inform therapeutic approaches for trauma, anxiety, and end-of-life care, improving mental health outcomes for individuals facing such challenges.

Expanding Scientific Understanding: NDE research pushes the boundaries of scientific exploration, encouraging us to rethink our understanding of consciousness and the nature of reality. This expanded knowledge can lead to discoveries and innovations in various fields.

In the future, NDE research may continue to bridge the gap between science, spirituality, and human experience, offering profound insights that have the potential to transform our understanding of life, death, and the ultimate purpose of our existence. It beckons us to embrace the limitless possibilities of the human journey and to create a future guided by love, compassion, and the pursuit of greater wisdom.

Chapter 21: NDEs and the Medical Community

How are NDEs perceived by the medical community?

Near-death experiences (NDEs) have long been a topic of fascination and contemplation in the medical community. However, they have also been met with skepticism due to their profound and often inexplicable nature.

Many medical professionals previously regarded NDEs as mere hallucinations or the byproducts of altered brain states during life-threatening situations. These experiences were often dismissed or attributed to the effects of anesthesia, drugs, or oxygen deprivation.

However, over the years, more medical practitioners have acknowledged the validity of NDEs, recognizing them as real and significant experiences reported by patients who have survived life-threatening situations. This shift in perception has prompted a more serious and scientific exploration of NDEs within the medical field.

What are the challenges of studying NDEs scientifically?

Scientifically studying NDEs presents a unique set of challenges. These experiences are deeply personal and subjective, making them difficult to measure and quantify using traditional research methods. Some of the challenges include the following:

Subjective Nature: NDEs are profoundly subjective experiences, and individuals often describe them in highly personal and symbolic terms. This subjectivity makes it challenging to establish a standardized framework for studying NDEs.

Lack of Control: NDEs occur spontaneously during life-threatening situations, and researchers cannot ethically induce such circumstances in controlled experiments. This lack of control hinders the ability to replicate NDEs under laboratory conditions.

Verifiability: While some elements of NDEs can be objectively verified, such as details of medical procedures, many aspects, such as encounters with deceased loved ones, are difficult to confirm independently.

Interdisciplinary Nature: The study of NDEs requires collaboration between medical professionals, neuroscientists, psychologists, and researchers from various fields. Bridging these interdisciplinary gaps can be challenging.

What new research methods are being developed to study NDEs?

Despite the challenges, innovative research methods are emerging to study NDEs more rigorously:

Prospective Studies: Researchers are conducting prospective studies by monitoring patients at high risk of experiencing NDEs, such as cardiac arrest patients; this allows for real-time data collection and analysis.

Advanced Brain Imaging: Neuroimaging techniques, such as functional magnetic resonance imaging (fMRI) and electroencephalography (EEG), are used to study brain activity during NDEs, providing insights into the neural correlates of these experiences.

Cross-Cultural Studies: Comparative studies across cultures explore how NDEs are perceived and interpreted globally, shedding light on the universal and culture-specific aspects of these experiences.

Longitudinal Research: Longitudinal studies are tracking individuals who have had NDEs over extended periods to assess the long-term effects on their mental health, well-being, and beliefs.

What are the implications of NDE research for medical practice?

NDE research has significant implications for medical practice, particularly in the fields of end-of-life care, mental health, and patient care:

Enhanced Compassion: Medical professionals who understand and acknowledge NDEs can provide more compassionate care to patients who have had these experiences, addressing their spiritual and emotional needs.

Improved End-of-Life Care: NDE research has highlighted the importance of providing support and comfort to patients facing death. Medical practitioners can integrate the lessons from NDEs into end-of-life care, promoting peaceful patient transitions.

Mental Health: Insights from NDE research can inform the development of therapeutic approaches that incorporate the profound lessons of love, compassion, and acceptance learned during NDEs, leading to more holistic mental health care.

Patient-Centered Care: Recognizing NDEs as legitimate and transformative experiences allows for more patient-centered care. Medical professionals can engage in open and empathetic dialogues with patients, fostering trust and understanding.

In the medical community, NDE research offers an opportunity to broaden our understanding of the human experience and to provide care that acknowledges the profound impact of these extraordinary journeys. By embracing the insights gained from NDEs, medical practitioners can contribute to a more compassionate and holistic approach to patient care and end-of-life support, ultimately enhancing the well-being of individuals facing life-threatening situations.

Chapter 22: NDEs and the Religious Community

How do different religions view NDEs?

Near-death experiences (NDEs) have a complex relationship with various religious traditions, each interpreting these profound encounters uniquely.

Christianity: In Christianity, NDEs are often seen as glimpses of the afterlife or encounters with divine beings, aligning with beliefs about heaven, angels, and the presence of God.

Islam: NDEs may be interpreted in Islam as moments of transition from earthly life to the hereafter, aligning with Islamic teachings about the akhirah (the afterlife) and encounters with angels.

Hinduism: In Hinduism, NDEs may be seen through the lens of reincarnation, reflecting beliefs about the soul's journey through multiple lives and encounters with deities or divine beings.

Buddhism: Buddhism, focusing on karma and rebirth, may view NDEs as part of the cycle of existence and a potential glimpse into the bardo (the intermediate state) between lives.

Indigenous Religions: Indigenous cultures often integrate NDEs into their spiritual beliefs, viewing these experiences as connections to the spirit world or encounters with ancestors.

How have NDEs influenced religious beliefs and practices throughout history?

Throughout history, NDEs have left an indelible mark on religious beliefs and practices:

Expansion of Spiritual Horizons: NDEs have expanded the horizons of religious understanding, challenging, and enriching theological perspectives on the afterlife, the nature of God, and the role of love and compassion.

Interfaith Dialogue: NDEs have prompted interfaith dialogue by highlighting common themes of love, interconnectedness, and spiritual growth across different religious traditions. This dialogue fosters greater understanding and tolerance among religious communities.

Reinterpretation of Texts: Some religious texts and scriptures have been reinterpreted in light of NDE insights, encouraging a more nuanced understanding of passages related to death, the soul, and the divine.

Spiritual Renewal: NDEs have ignited spiritual renewal movements, inspiring individuals to seek a deeper and more personal relationship with the divine. This renewal often emphasizes the transformative power of love and compassion.

What roles do NDEs play in contemporary religious communities?

In contemporary religious communities, NDEs play several roles:

Confirmation of Faith: For some individuals, NDEs confirm their pre-existing religious beliefs, reinforcing their faith in the existence of an afterlife, divine beings, or spiritual realms.

Spiritual Catalyst: NDEs serve as spiritual catalysts, inspiring individuals to deepen their religious practices, engage in prayer or meditation, and seek a more profound connection with the divine.

Interfaith Understanding: NDEs promote interfaith understanding by highlighting the universal themes of love, compassion, and interconnectedness shared among different religious traditions.

Support in Grief: NDEs can solace those experiencing grief and loss by suggesting the continuation of consciousness beyond death and the possibility of reunion with loved ones.

How can NDEs help to bridge the gap between different religions?

NDEs have the potential to serve as bridges between different religions by emphasizing universal themes and values:

Common Ground: NDEs underscore the common ground shared by various religions—the importance of love, compassion, and spiritual growth. Recognizing these shared values can foster greater interfaith harmony.

Interfaith Dialogue: NDEs inspire interfaith dialogue, encouraging individuals from different religious backgrounds to discuss and explore the profound spiritual truths revealed by these experiences.

Tolerance and Respect: By acknowledging the validity of NDEs in different religious contexts, individuals can promote greater tolerance and respect for diverse beliefs and practices.

Shared Mysteries: NDEs remind us that the mysteries of life, death, and the afterlife are shared by all of humanity, transcending religious boundaries. This recognition can promote humility and unity among religious communities.

In contemporary society, NDEs offer a unique opportunity to foster greater understanding, tolerance, and interconnectedness among religious traditions. By recognizing the common threads that run through these extraordinary experiences, individuals from diverse backgrounds can come together to pursue more significant spiritual growth, love, and compassion for all humanity.

Chapter 23: NDEs and the Media

How have NDEs been portrayed in the media?

Near-death experiences (NDEs) have captured the media's imagination for decades, often portrayed in both sensationalized and contemplative ways. These portrayals have evolved, reflecting changing perspectives and societal attitudes.

Early Sensationalism: In the early days of NDE reporting, the media often sensationalized these experiences, framing them as supernatural phenomena or "miraculous" events. These stories sometimes needed more depth and accuracy, focusing on the sensational aspects rather than the profound insights.

Documentary and Investigative Journalism: As interest in NDEs grew, documentary filmmakers and investigative journalists explored these experiences in more detail. They sought to present NDEs as meaningful and potentially transformative encounters, often featuring interviews with experiencers and experts.

Scientific Inquiry: With the increasing recognition of NDEs in the scientific community, some media outlets have shifted towards a more objective and research-oriented approach. They cover studies, interviews with scientists, and discussions on NDEs' neuroscientific and psychological aspects.

Diverse Perspectives: More recently, the media has embraced diverse perspectives on NDEs, featuring stories from people of different backgrounds, cultures, and belief systems. This inclusivity highlights the universal nature of NDE themes.

What impact has the media had on public awareness of NDEs?

The media has played a significant role in raising public awareness of NDEs:

Increased Recognition: Media coverage has contributed to greater recognition and acceptance of NDEs as accurate and meaningful experiences, dispelling earlier dismissals of them as mere hallucinations.

Education: Documentaries, news reports, and feature articles have educated the public about the profound and transformative nature of NDEs, fostering a deeper understanding of the experiences.

Scientific Engagement: Media coverage of NDE research has drawn attention to the scientific exploration of these experiences, encouraging public interest in NDEs' neurological and psychological aspects.

Supportive Communities: NDE-related media coverage has helped connect experiencers with supportive communities where they can share their stories and find understanding and validation.

What are the challenges and opportunities of presenting NDEs accurately and respectfully in the media?

Presenting NDEs in the media comes with both challenges and opportunities:

Challenges:

Sensationalism: The media may be tempted to sensationalize NDEs for higher viewership or readership; this can distort the experiences and trivialize their profound nature.

Accuracy: Ensuring the accuracy of NDE portrayals can be challenging due to the subjective nature of these experiences. Misrepresentations may lead to misunderstandings.

Balancing Skepticism: Striking a balance between skepticism and open-mindedness in media coverage is essential. While skepticism can be healthy, it should not dismiss NDEs without consideration.

Opportunities:

Education: The media can educate the public about NDEs, fostering empathy and understanding for those who have had these experiences.

Empowerment: Media coverage empowers experiencers to share their stories, helping them find validation and contributing to their emotional healing.

Science Communication: The media can bridge scientific research and the public, explaining complex concepts and findings in accessible ways.

Promoting Dialogue: NDE coverage can encourage open dialogue among viewers or readers, sparking discussions about the nature of consciousness, spirituality, and the afterlife.

How can the media help to promote a deeper understanding of NDEs?

The media can promote a deeper understanding of NDEs by:

Balanced Reporting: Maintaining a balance between skepticism and open-mindedness in reporting, allowing for diverse perspectives and experiences to be shared.

Respectful Language: Using respectful and empathetic language when describing NDEs and the individuals who have had them, recognizing these encounters' profound and deeply personal nature.

Scientific Engagement: Covering the latest scientific research on NDEs and interviewing experts to provide viewers or readers with a well-rounded view of the subject.

Diverse Perspectives: Featuring stories from various NDE experiencers, including those from different cultural, religious, and philosophical backgrounds.

Education and Resources: Providing viewers or readers with educational resources and references to further explore the topic of NDEs, encouraging a deeper understanding.

Through responsible and compassionate reporting, the media has the potential to contribute positively to the public's understanding of NDEs, fostering empathy, curiosity, and a broader appreciation for the profound mysteries of human consciousness and existence.

Chapter 25: NDEs and Popular Culture

How have NDEs been portrayed in popular culture, such as movies, TV shows, books, and music?

Near-death experiences (NDEs) have found their way into the creative expressions of popular culture, weaving threads of wonder and contemplation into various art forms:

Movies: NDEs have been a recurring theme in cinema, with films like "Flatliners" and "Hereafter" exploring the mysteries of life, death, and what lies beyond. These movies often portray the awe and transformation experienced by NDErs.

TV Shows: Television series like "The OA" and episodes of shows like "Grey's Anatomy" have delved into NDEs, capturing the intrigue of these experiences and their potential impact on characters' lives.

Books: NDEs have inspired numerous books, both fiction and nonfiction. Authors have penned captivating stories of individuals who journey to the brink of death and return with profound insights, changing their lives forever.

Music: Musicians have woven NDE themes into their songs, exploring the emotions and spiritual dimensions of these experiences. Lyrics often touch on themes of light, love, and transcendence.

What impact has popular culture had on public understanding of NDEs?

Popular culture has played a pivotal role in shaping public understanding of NDEs:

Awareness: Movies, TV shows, books, and music have raised awareness of NDEs, introducing these experiences to a broader audience and sparking curiosity.

Empathy: NDE portrayals in popular culture have evoked empathy for experiencers, fostering a deeper appreciation for their journeys' emotional and spiritual aspects.

Reflection: These creative works encourage audiences to reflect on profound questions about life, death, consciousness, and the nature of reality, expanding the scope of their contemplations.

More profound Interest: Popular culture has ignited a deeper interest in NDEs, prompting viewers and readers to seek out nonfiction resources and accounts to learn more about these experiences.

What are the challenges and opportunities of presenting NDEs accurately and respectfully in popular culture?

Presenting NDEs in popular culture presents both challenges and opportunities:

Challenges:

Simplification: There is a risk of oversimplifying NDEs to fit them into the storytelling constraints, potentially sacrificing the depth and complexity of these experiences.

Sensationalism: Some portrayals may prioritize dramatic elements for entertainment value, potentially sensationalizing NDEs and misrepresenting their profound nature.

Misconceptions: Popular culture can perpetuate misconceptions about NDEs, leading to misunderstandings and reinforcing stereotypes.

Opportunities:

Inspiration: Accurate and respectful portrayals can inspire individuals to explore NDEs further, fostering a deeper understanding of these transformative experiences.

Conversation Starter: Popular culture can catalyze conversations about NDEs, encouraging viewers and readers to engage with the subject matter meaningfully.

Empathy and Compassion: Thoughtful portrayals can evoke empathy and compassion, helping audiences connect with NDEs' emotional and spiritual aspects.

How can popular culture help to promote a deeper understanding of NDEs?

Popular culture can promote a deeper understanding of NDEs by:

Research and Accuracy: Ensuring that creators of movies, TV shows, books, and music conduct thorough research to accurately represent NDEs, their emotional impact, and the various elements that experiencers report.

Realistic Complexity: Encouraging the portrayal of NDEs with the depth and complexity they deserve, acknowledging the transformative and multi-dimensional aspects of these experiences.

Education: Accompanying fictional portrayals with educational resources, references, or interviews with experts in the field can provide audiences with a more comprehensive understanding of NDEs.

Diverse Voices: Encouraging diverse voices and perspectives in popular culture representations, reflecting the range of individuals who have had NDEs across different backgrounds, cultures, and belief systems.

Through thoughtful and respectful representations, popular culture can bridge the extraordinary realm of NDEs and the broader public, fostering empathy, curiosity, and a deeper appreciation for the profound mysteries of human consciousness and existence.

Chapter 26: NDEs and the Nature of Consciousness

Near-death experiences (NDEs) have the remarkable capacity to peel back the layers of the unknown, inviting us to contemplate the profound mysteries surrounding the nature of consciousness:

What do NDEs teach us about the nature of consciousness?

NDEs offer tantalizing glimpses into the expansive realm of consciousness. They suggest that consciousness may transcend the physical body's limitations and the confines of everyday perception. Experiencers often describe heightened awareness, enhanced sensory perception, and a profound sense of interconnectedness with the universe. NDEs illuminate that consciousness is far more intricate and expansive than we might have imagined.

Is consciousness independent of the brain?

NDEs challenge the conventional view that consciousness is solely a product of brain activity. During these experiences, some individuals report vivid perceptions and lucid thoughts even when their brains show little to no measurable activity; this raises profound questions about the relationship between consciousness and the brain.

While NDEs do not definitively prove that consciousness is independent of the brain, they do suggest the possibility that consciousness may exist beyond the confines of our physical bodies. They invite us to explore the hypothesis that consciousness is a fundamental aspect of the universe, not limited to the neural networks of our brains.

Can consciousness survive the death of the body?

NDEs provide a tantalizing glimpse into consciousness's potential survival beyond the physical body's death. Many NDErs report leaving their bodies, often observing medical procedures from an out-of-body perspective. They describe encounters with deceased loved ones and sometimes venture into otherworldly realms.

While NDEs do not offer conclusive proof of the afterlife, they prompt us to consider that consciousness may endure beyond the cessation of biological functions. These experiences invite us to explore the possibility that death may not be the final chapter but rather a transition to another state of existence.

What are the implications of NDEs for our understanding of ourselves and our place in the universe?

NDEs profoundly affect our understanding of ourselves and our place in the vast cosmos. They challenge our conventional beliefs and encourage a more expansive worldview:

Connectedness: NDEs highlight the interconnectedness of all living beings, emphasizing themes of love, compassion, and unity. They invite us to recognize our shared humanity and the interdependence of all life on Earth.

Transcendence: NDEs suggest that we are more than our physical bodies. They encourage us to explore the transcendent aspects of our existence and the potential for personal growth and spiritual evolution.

Mysteries of the Universe: These experiences prompt us to contemplate the universe's secrets, including the nature of reality, the existence of other dimensions, and the possibility of intelligent cosmic forces.

Life's Purpose: NDEs often lead experiencers to reevaluate their life's purpose and priorities, emphasizing the importance of love, compassion, and meaningful connections with others.

In Near-Death Experiences, consciousness emerges as a profound enigma, offering us glimpses of a reality that transcends our everyday understanding. These experiences invite us to embark on a journey of exploration, prompting us to ask questions that reach beyond the boundaries of our current knowledge and inspiring us to contemplate the nature of consciousness, our place in the universe, and the limitless possibilities that lie beyond the horizon of our current understanding.

Chapter 27: NDEs and the Afterlife

Near-death experiences (NDEs) serve as ethereal windows into the mysteries of the afterlife, urging us to contemplate the profound nature of existence beyond the threshold of death:

What do NDEs tell us about the afterlife?

NDEs offer compelling insights into the afterlife, painting vivid pictures of what may lie beyond our mortal existence. Many experiencers describe encounters with a radiant light or a realm of extraordinary beauty and tranquility. They often meet deceased loved ones, angelic beings, or guides conveying unconditional love and acceptance. These glimpses of the afterlife suggest a profound love, understanding, and peace-filled realm.

Is there life after death?

NDEs strongly suggest the possibility of life after death. Experiencers frequently describe their consciousness persisting beyond the point of clinical death, even when their bodies show no signs of life; this leads us to consider the hypothesis that death may be a transition rather than an end—a journey of consciousness into a different state of existence.

While NDEs do not provide definitive proof of life after death, they invite us to explore this tantalizing possibility, igniting our imaginations and challenging the conventional boundaries of mortality.

What is the nature of the afterlife?

The nature of the afterlife, as depicted in NDEs, is characterized by profound and universal themes:

Love and Light: Experiencers consistently describe encounters with an overwhelming, loving light that radiates compassion, understanding, and acceptance. This light is often associated with a sense of homecoming.

Transcendence: NDEs transcend the limitations of our physical world, revealing a realm where communication is telepathic, perception is heightened, and time and space appear fluid; this suggests that the afterlife may be a realm of expanded consciousness.

Reunion: Many NDErs encounter deceased loved ones who welcome them with open arms. Deep emotional connections and profound joy mark these reunions.

Life Review: The afterlife often includes a life review—a panoramic examination of one's life experiences. This review is not judgmental but an opportunity for personal growth and reflection.

What are the implications of NDEs for our understanding of death and dying?

NDEs hold profound implications for our understanding of death and the dying process:

Easing Fear of Death: NDE accounts often describe a peaceful and loving transition from life to the afterlife. These narratives can offer comfort and solace to those facing the end of life, helping to alleviate the fear of death.

Reframing Death: NDEs invite us to reframe death as a natural and transformative process rather than an ultimate end. This shift in perspective can lead to a more peaceful acceptance of mortality.

Embracing Compassion: NDEs emphasize the importance of love, compassion, and meaningful connections with others. They encourage us to prioritize these values and interactions with those dying.

Exploration of Consciousness: NDEs prompt us to explore the nature of consciousness and its potential beyond the physical body. They encourage us to explore the relationship between consciousness and the universe.

In the presence of Near-Death Experiences, the concept of the afterlife emerges as a profound enigma, a tantalizing glimpse of what may await us beyond the threshold of mortality. These experiences challenge us to reconsider our understanding of life, death, and the enduring mysteries of existence, inviting us to explore the transformative potential of love, compassion, and the eternal journey of the human soul.

Chapter 28: NDEs and the Meaning of Life

Near-death experiences (NDEs) are profound journeys into the heart of existence, guiding us toward a deeper understanding of life's purpose and the profound meaning woven into the tapestry of our existence:

What do NDEs teach us about the meaning of life?

NDEs illuminate the profound meaning embedded in our human journey. They often reveal that life is a sacred and purposeful experience, brimming with opportunities for growth, love, and connection. Experiencers frequently describe a profound sense of clarity about the purpose of life, emphasizing the significance of love, compassion, and spiritual evolution.

Why are we here?

NDEs suggest that we are here to learn, grow, and evolve as spiritual beings. These experiences often convey that life on Earth is a unique opportunity for our souls to expand and deepen their understanding. We are here to experience the rich tapestry of human emotions, learn from our joys and struggles, and cultivate love, empathy, and wisdom.

What is our purpose in life?

The purpose of life, as illuminated by NDEs, is to embrace the transformative power of love. Experiencers frequently report that they are shown the importance of love—the love we give and receive. They emphasize that our purpose is to nurture our connections with others, to show kindness, and to leave a positive mark on the world.

NDEs also suggest that our purpose extends beyond the self. We are here to contribute to humanity's collective growth, help each other on our journeys, and foster greater unity and interconnectedness.

How can we live more meaningful and fulfilling lives?

NDEs inspire us to live more meaningful and fulfilling lives by offering profound insights:

Embrace Love: Love is at the core of a meaningful life. NDEs emphasize the importance of expressing love to ourselves and others. Acts of kindness, empathy, and compassion enrich our lives and contribute to our sense of purpose.

Value Relationships: Building meaningful relationships and connections with others is a fundamental aspect of a fulfilling life. NDEs encourage us to prioritize and nurture our relationships with care and understanding.

Live Authentically: Authenticity and aligning with our true selves are vital to a meaningful life. NDEs often reveal that embracing one's essence is critical to finding purpose and fulfillment.

Seek Inner Growth: NDEs underscore the significance of spiritual growth and personal development. Embracing inner growth and self-discovery opportunities can lead to a more profound sense of purpose and fulfillment.

Practice Gratitude: NDEs frequently highlight the importance of gratitude. Being mindful of the beauty and blessings in our lives fosters a sense of contentment and enhances our overall well-being.

In the presence of Near-Death Experiences, life's meaning unfolds as a luminous tapestry woven with the threads of love, connection, and spiritual growth. These profound journeys remind us that our purpose on Earth is to embrace love's transformative power, nurture our relationships with others, and cultivate a life that radiates meaning and fulfillment.

Chapter 29: NDEs and the Future of Humanity

Near-death experiences (NDEs) serve as profound beacons of insight, guiding us toward a future infused with compassion, love, and transformative potential.

What do NDEs teach us about the future of humanity?

NDEs offer glimpses of a future for humanity infused with profound spiritual wisdom. They reveal a vision of a world where love, compassion, and interconnectedness are valued above all else. Experiencers often return with a sense of purpose, a heightened awareness of the impact of their actions, and a deep commitment to contributing to a more compassionate and loving world.

Are we on the right track?

NDEs serve as poignant reminders that we can redirect our path toward a more enlightened and compassionate future. They suggest that we may have strayed from a deeper understanding of our interconnectedness and the importance of love, but they also offer hope that we can realign with these values.

What can we do to create a better future for ourselves and future generations?

NDEs illuminate a path forward, offering profound insights into how we can shape a better future:

Embrace Love: NDEs emphasize that love is the cornerstone of a better future. We can prioritize love in all our interactions, nurturing empathy, understanding, and kindness toward one another.

Practice Compassion: Compassion is a guiding principle for a brighter future. NDEs encourage us to extend compassion to all beings, recognizing that we are interconnected in our shared human journey.

Foster Unity: We can work to break down barriers of division and embrace our shared humanity. NDEs suggest that unity and understanding are essential for a more harmonious world.

Heal the World: NDE experiencers often return with a profound commitment to healing the world. We can follow in their footsteps by serving and contributing to improving society and the planet.

Live with Purpose: NDEs underscore the importance of living with purpose and intention. We can cultivate lives that align with our deepest values and strive to impact the world positively.

How can NDEs help us to become a more compassionate and loving species?

NDEs are catalysts for transformation, offering us the following ways to become a more compassionate and loving species:

Inspiration: NDEs inspire us with stories of individuals who have undergone profound transformations through their experiences. These stories encourage us to seek our personal growth and greater compassion.

Education: NDEs educate us about the transformative power of love and compassion. They teach us that these qualities have the potential to heal wounds, bridge divides, and create a more harmonious world.

Collective Healing: By sharing NDE stories and their messages of love and unity, we can contribute to collective healing and inspire others to embrace a more compassionate way of life.

Reflection: NDEs invite us to reflect on our own lives and values. They encourage us to consider how we can align our actions with the principles of love and compassion.

Global Impact: When individuals commit to living with greater love and compassion, the ripple effects can extend far beyond their immediate circles, ultimately contributing to a more compassionate and loving world.

In the presence of Near-Death Experiences, we glimpse a future where love and compassion are the guiding principles of humanity. These profound journeys remind us that we have the power to create a brighter future by embracing love, practicing compassion, fostering unity, and living with purpose. The future of humanity, as illuminated by NDEs, holds the promise of a world where our collective hearts shine with a radiant light of love, compassion, and understanding.

Chapter 30: Resources and Further Reading

Here, I offer a guiding light, illuminating the path to additional resources and further reading so you may continue your transformative trip:

Books That Illuminate the Afterlife:

"Beyond the Light" by P.M.H. Atwater: An exploration of various types of NDEs, shedding light on the transformative potential of these experiences.

"The Light Beyond" by Raymond A. Moody Jr.: Written by the pioneer who coined the term "Near-Death Experience," this book delves into the spiritual dimensions of NDEs.

"Into the Light" by John Lerma: A compassionate guide that explores the profound spiritual aspects of NDEs, offering insights into the soul's journey beyond.

Spiritual Enlightenment and Self-Discovery:

"The Power of Now" by Eckhart Tolle: A transformative classic that guides readers toward living in the present moment, unveiling the peace and enlightenment within.

"The Untethered Soul" by Michael A. Singer: An exploration of the limitless potential of the human soul and the path to spiritual freedom.

"A New Earth" by Eckhart Tolle: A profound examination of ego, consciousness, and the collective awakening of humanity, offering insights into personal and planetary transformation.

Online Resources:

Near-Death Experience Research Foundation (NDERF): A comprehensive online resource offering a vast collection of NDE accounts, research articles, and insights from experts in the field.

International Association for Near-Death Studies (IANDS): A global organization dedicated to the study and support of those who have had NDEs, offering conferences, publications, and a wealth of online resources.

Spiritual Teachers and Guides: Explore the teachings of contemporary spiritual leaders like Deepak Chopra, Thich Nhat Hanh, and Eckhart Tolle, whose wisdom guides seekers toward profound spiritual understanding.

Communities of Support and Sharing:

Online Forums and Support Groups: Engage with online communities where individuals share their NDE experiences, fostering connection and understanding among those who have undergone similar journeys.

Local Spiritual Centers: Seek out spiritual centers and communities in your area where you can participate in discussions, workshops, and meditation sessions, fostering a sense of belonging and shared spiritual exploration.

In your continued pursuit of wisdom and spiritual growth, these resources serve as beacons, illuminating the path toward a deeper understanding of NDEs and the profound mysteries of existence. As you delve further into these realms, may your journey be one of discovery, enlightenment, and boundless love.

Conclusion

In the pages of this book, we have embarked on a remarkable journey through the profound and mystical realm of Near-Death Experiences (NDEs). We have delved into the depths of these extraordinary encounters, seeking to unravel the mysteries they hold and the wisdom they offer. As our journey nears its conclusion, let us reflect on the key points we have discovered:

We have learned that NDEs are not mere glimpses into the unknown but profound encounters with the divine, offering us insights into the nature of consciousness, the afterlife, and the meaning of our existence.

NDEs have shown us that the afterlife is a realm of boundless love, light, and interconnectedness. They suggest that consciousness may transcend the confines of the physical body, offering hope that life persists beyond the threshold of death.

These experiences have taught us that our purpose on Earth is to embrace love, nurture compassion, and foster unity. They invite us to live with intention, authenticity, and a commitment to positively impacting the world.

As we conclude this journey, let us recognize that this book is not merely a collection of stories and insights but a call to action for each of us to explore our understanding of NDEs and the afterlife. It invites us to contemplate the profound questions of existence, consciousness, and our place in the universe.

But it is also a vision for a future in which NDEs are more widely accepted and understood. It is a future in which the lessons of NDEs are not confined to the pages of books but are used to shape a better world for all.

Imagine a world where love and compassion are the guiding principles of humanity, where unity and understanding bridge the divides that separate us. Picture a world where the transformative power of NDEs is harnessed to heal wounds, foster connection, and create a more harmonious existence.

This is the world that NDEs beckon us toward—a world where we recognize our shared humanity, where we prioritize love above all else, and where we commit to living lives of purpose and meaning.

As we bid farewell to this journey through the mysteries of NDEs, let us carry the wisdom of these experiences in our hearts. Let us become ambassadors of love and compassion, spreading their transformative light to every corner of our lives and world.

Near-death experiences have woven threads of hope, illumination, and profound understanding. May we carry these threads forward, creating a future where the lessons of NDEs guide us toward a world filled with love, compassion, and boundless possibility.

Printed in Great Britain
by Amazon